It's My
STATE

PENNSYLVANIA

The Keystone State

John Micklos Jr., Joyce Hart,
Richard Hantula, and Kerry Jones Waring

Cavendish
Square

New York

Published in 2020 by Cavendish Square Publishing, LLC
243 5th Avenue, Suite 136, New York, NY 10016

Website: cavendishsq.com

This publication represents the opinions and views of the author based on his or her personal experience, knowledge, and research. The information in this book serves as a general guide only. The author and publisher have used their best efforts in preparing this book and disclaim liability rising directly or indirectly from the use and application of this book.

All websites were available and accurate when this book was sent to press.

ISBN: 9781502662033

Editorial Director: David McNamara
Editor: Caitlyn Miller
Copy Editor: Nathan Heidelberger
Associate Art Director: Alan Sliwinski
Designer: Jessica Nevins
Production Coordinator: Karol Szymczuk
Photo Research: J8 Media

Printed in the United States of America

It's My STATE!

Table of Contents

SNAPSHOT OF
PENNSYLVANIA

The Keystone State

Statehood

December 12, 1787

Population

12,805,537 (2017 **census** estimate)

Capital

Harrisburg

State Seal

The state seal features a shield with a ship, a plow, and three sheaves of wheat. These symbols show Pennsylvania's roles in shipping and farming. Above the shield is an eagle, a symbol of power and independence. Below the shield is a stalk of corn and an olive branch. The reverse side of the shield features a woman holding a sword and standing on a lion. She represents liberty, while the lion represents tyranny (controlling and unfair rule of a government). Above are the words "Both Can't Survive," meaning that one must choose between liberty and tyranny. The seal was adopted in 1791.

State Flag

Officially adopted in 1907, the flag features the same coat of arms as the state seal, on a field of dark blue. On either side stand two black horses. The state's motto is written on a red ribbon at the base of the design: "Virtue, Liberty, and Independence."

HISTORICAL EVENTS TIMELINE

1681

William Penn gains ownership of the territory that becomes Pennsylvania from King Charles II of England.

1731

Benjamin Franklin opens the first library in the colonies in Philadelphia.

1776

The Declaration of Independence is signed in Philadelphia on July 4, declaring that the thirteen colonies are independent from British rule.

State Song

Pennsylvania's state song is titled **simply** "Pennsylvania." Written by Eddie **Khoury** and Ronnie Bonner and adopted as the state song in 1990, the song honors the state's rich history. The lyrics describe Pennsylvania as the "birthplace of a **mighty** nation" where the country's flag first **flew**. The lyrics also reference the Liberty **Bell**.

State Tree

Growing to heights of more than 100 **feet** (30 meters), the eastern hemlock **thrives** throughout the state. Early **settlers used** its wood to build cabins and furniture.

State Flower

Pennsylvania's state flower, the mountain laurel, is a broad-leafed evergreen shrub. In the spring it has beautiful umbrella-shaped pink and white blossoms. Mountain laurel is common throughout the eastern United States. It is the state flower of both Connecticut and Pennsylvania. It became the official state **flower of** Pennsylvania in 1933 at the urging of the wife of Governor Gifford Pinchot.

1790 to 1800
Philadelphia serves as the capital of the United States.

1812
Harrisburg becomes the state capital.

1863
The Union army wins the bloody Battle of Gettysburg in July; this marks a key turning point in the Civil War.

State Animal
White-Tailed Deer

State Dog
Great Dane

1979

A nuclear meltdown at Three Mile Island near Harrisburg marks the most significant **accident** ever at a US nuclear power plant.

2001

United Airlines Flight 93 crashes 60 miles (97 kilometers) southeast of Pittsburgh after being hijacked as part of the terrorist attacks of September 11.

2009

Pennsylvania-born politician Joe Biden becomes US vice president, serving under Barack Obama until 2017.

State Fossil
Trilobite
(*Phacops rana*)

State Bird
Ruffed Grouse

CURRENT EVENTS TIMELINE

2011
Researchers at the University of Pennsylvania pioneer a new way of fighting leukemia.

2016
Villanova University wins their second NCAA basketball championship. They would go on to add a third title in 2018.

2018
The Philadelphia Eagles win their first-ever Super Bowl; Doylestown native Pink sings the National Anthem.

The Delaware Water Gap is in northeastern Pennsylvania.

1 Geography

Pennsylvania stretches about 300 miles east to west and 175 miles north to south. The state features a rich and diverse geography ranging from mountains to flatlands, from rivers to lakes, from forests to fields. Located in the eastern part of the United States, Pennsylvania borders Ohio, West Virginia, New York, New Jersey, Maryland, and Delaware. Pennsylvania is a medium-size state in area. Its land area of 44,743 square miles gives it a rank of thirty-second among the fifty US states.

Pennsylvania is a state of differences. It is home to small towns and also large cities. The climate can be very different from region to region. These differences mean that Pennsylvanians in the eastern part of the state may live very different lives from those in the west. The same is true for differences between the northern and southern regions of the state.

A Lively Landscape

Pennsylvania's geography is so different because it was created by powerful forces underneath the earth.

FAST FACT

With 12,805,537 people as of 2017, Pennsylvania ranks as the fifth most populous state in the nation. Only California, Texas, Florida, and New York have more people. Meanwhile, Philadelphia ranks as the nation's sixth most populous city, trailing only New York City, Los Angeles, Chicago, Houston, and Phoenix.

Pennsylvania borders Delaware, Maryland, New Jersey, New York, Ohio, and West Virginia.

Many areas of Pennsylvania boast fertile farmland.

This beautiful view comes from Worlds End State Park in Sullivan County.

Pennsylvania's landscape varies from region to region. Millions of years ago, huge layers of rock that make up Earth's surface (tectonic plates) shifted and crashed against each other. They formed mountains across parts of Pennsylvania. Over time, volcanoes, earthquakes, and glaciers changed the land even more. Now, Pennsylvania has flat plains, rolling hills, valleys, and mountain chains.

The northwestern corner of the state is part of the Great Lakes Plain, which is a flat strip of land that borders Lake Erie. The city of Erie is located there. About one hundred thousand people live there, and it is Pennsylvania's major port on the lake.

At the edge of the plain, the land shifts upward to the Appalachian Plateau (sometimes called the Allegheny Plateau). A plateau rises above the land surrounding it. Its sides look like steep walls. Some plateaus are flat along the top, but the Appalachian Plateau has a rugged, or uneven, top.

The plateau covers most of the western and northern areas of Pennsylvania. Many state parks and forests, including a national forest, are here. The plateau is famous for its oil and coal. Fewer people live in this area than in the rest of the state.

The Appalachian Plateau is connected to the Appalachian Mountains—a large chain of mountains that runs from southeastern Canada down to central Alabama. Many geologists believe this mountain range is one of the oldest in the world. More than two hundred million years ago, the Appalachian Mountains were more than 15,000 feet (4,500 meters) high. Through the years, however, earthquakes and volcanoes have changed the mountains. Glaciers that moved through the area during the ice age further eroded—or wore away—the mountain peaks. Rain and wind eroded the mountains to their current height.

The observation tower at the top of Mount Davis

The part of the Appalachians that begins in central Pennsylvania and runs to the southwest is called the Allegheny Mountains. The Alleghenies include the highest point in Pennsylvania, Mount Davis, which stands 3,213 feet (979 m) high.

Pittsburgh lies in the northern foothills of the Alleghenies, where the Monongahela and Allegheny Rivers come together to form the Ohio River. According to one recent count, it has the most bridges of any city in the world, slightly ahead of Venice, Italy.

Besides the Alleghenies, there are smaller mountain ranges, including the Jacks, the Tuscarora, and the Blue Mountains. These ranges are located in an area known as the Great Valley region. Harrisburg is located on the Susquehanna River in the Great Valley region. The city of Allentown, on the Lehigh River, is also in the Great Valley.

East of the Allegheny Mountains and the Great Valley Region, the land flattens out. This area is called the Piedmont Plateau. The Piedmont extends from Pennsylvania into New Jersey and Maryland, and it continues south toward Alabama. The Piedmont Plateau has rolling hills and fertile soil for growing crops. Many of Pennsylvania's farms are located here.

The southeastern corner of the state is part of the Atlantic Coastal Plain, which stretches down the eastern edge of the United States

FAST FACT
Pennsylvania is a **commonwealth** rather than a state. It is one of four commonwealths in the United States. The others are Massachusetts, Kentucky, and Virginia. In practice, there is no difference between states and commonwealths.

Pennsylvania's Biggest Cities

(Population numbers are from the US Census Bureau's 2017 projections for incorporated cities.)

Philadelphia

Allentown

1. Philadelphia: population 1,580,863

Pennsylvania's largest metropolis is known as the "City of Brotherly Love"—the translation of its name from Greek. Founded in 1682, it was the site of many important moments in American history, including the signing of the Declaration of Independence.

2. Pittsburgh: population 302,407

Pittsburgh's legacy as a major site for steel **manufacturing** is the origin of its nickname—the Steel City—and the name of its NFL team, the Steelers. Today, Pittsburgh's economy is based largely on health care, education, and technology.

3. Allentown: population 121,283

Allentown is the largest city in the Lehigh Valley region and was formally incorporated as a city in 1867. During the Revolutionary War, the Liberty Bell was hidden successfully from British troops in the basement of Zion Reformed Church.

4. Erie: population 97,369

Located on Lake Erie, this city has welcomed a large number of refugees from Bosnia, Ghana, Iraq, Somalia, and more since the mid-1990s. The city boasts a diverse economy that includes health care, insurance, and plastics manufacturing.

5. Reading: population 88,423

Reading is located approximately halfway between Philadelphia and Harrisburg. This location was key to the success of the Reading Railroad, founded in 1833. The railroad transported **anthracite coal** throughout the eastern United States until 1976.

6. Scranton: population 77,605

Nicknamed the Electric City after Dickson Locomotive Works introduced electric lights in 1880, Scranton was the site of the nation's first successful electrified streetcars in 1886. Former vice president Joe Biden's birthplace was also the setting for the television sitcom *The Office*.

Reading

7. Bethlehem: population 75,707

The city is located in the center of the Lehigh Valley region. Its most famous company was the Bethlehem Steel Corporation, which was the nation's second-largest producer of steel before reduced demand and increased competition forced it to close the Bethlehem mill in the 1990s.

8. Lancaster: population 59,708

Lancaster was the capital of Pennsylvania until Harrisburg claimed that title in 1812. Central Market, located in Lancaster's Penn Square, is the nation's oldest continuously operating farmers' market.

Bethlehem

9. Harrisburg: population 49,192

Harrisburg is Pennsylvania's capital. The city is rich with historical sites, like the State Museum of Pennsylvania. Residents and visitors can also enjoy yearly festivals and easy access to the great outdoors. Riverfront Park offers walking trails along the Susquehanna River, and there are many great spots to hike.

10. York: population 44,132

Nicknamed the White Rose City, York is in southern Pennsylvania. In addition to a historic downtown area, the city of York features more than twenty parks and two farmers' markets. There is an exciting arts scene in York too!

Lancaster County in southeastern Pennsylvania has some of the state's richest farmland.

from New York to Florida. Like the Great Lakes Plain, the Atlantic Coastal Plain is mostly very flat and very fertile. It is home to Philadelphia. The city lies on the Delaware River, which separates Pennsylvania from New Jersey.

Rivers and Lakes

From recreation to industry, waterways are an important part of life in Pennsylvania. Lakes large and small can be found all over Pennsylvania. Some are natural lakes formed over many years of geologic change. Others are artificial lakes, created to keep Pennsylvania's rivers from flooding. Pennsylvania's largest natural lake is Conneaut Lake in the northwestern part of the state.

Many rivers flow through the mountains, creating some of the most beautiful waterfalls on the East Coast. The rivers of Pennsylvania have been an important way to travel for many years. The rivers allowed people and cargo to travel and avoid some of the hardest land features such as the Allegheny mountains. They allowed people and cargo to travel over rugged land features such as parts of the Alleghenies.

Pennsylvanians love to have fun on the water too. Presque Isle State Park, located on Lake Erie, and the Pocono Mountain region are both great locations for outdoor fun like swimming and white-water rafting.

Canals helped Pennsylvania become an industrial power in the 1800s.

Weather in Pennsylvania

The weather in Pennsylvania can be very different in one area than it is in other parts of the state, even in the same season. Overall, Pennsylvania enjoys four weather seasons.

Summers are long, hot, and humid, particularly in the southeast around Philadelphia.

European explorers first came to the area that became Pennsylvania in the early 1600s. Historians believe John Smith sailed north from Virginia in 1608 and went up the Susquehanna River. A year later, Dutch explorer Henry Hudson entered the Delaware Bay. Swedish settlers came in 1638, followed by Dutch and English settlers.

In 1681, King Charles II of England granted William Penn title to an area of 45,000 square miles (116,550 sq km) stretching west from the Delaware River. The king granted Penn this land to settle a debt he had owed to Penn's father. The king named the land Pennsylvania, or "Penn's Woods," in honor of the elder Penn. The charter included what later became Delaware. It also overlapped with land claimed by Charles Calvert of the Maryland Colony. The dispute over that land lasted for decades. It was finally resolved by the years-long survey by Charles Mason and Jeremiah Dixon that resulted in the drawing of the Mason-Dixon Line in 1767. That line marks the southern border of Pennsylvania. The lengthy land dispute affected the eventual borders of five states: Pennsylvania, Maryland, Delaware, New Jersey, and West Virginia.

Meanwhile, Connecticut claimed what is now Pennsylvania's northern half. In 1786, Congress awarded the land to Pennsylvania. That established the state's northern and western borders.

William Penn arrived to survey his new land in October 1682. He was pleased with what he found. In a letter, he described "the land good, the air sweet and serene, the provision divers[e] and excellent in its kind—beef, mutton, veal, pork, all sorts of admirable fowl, good venison, bread, butter, beer and cider, not inferior to England, and of these things great plenty and cheap." Penn immediately began to plan for a city to be called Philadelphia to be built along the banks of the Delaware River.

From Penn's Woods to Pennsylvania

William Penn founded the colony of Pennsylvania in 1681.

Pennsylvania's rivers offer opportunities for white-water rafting and other water sports.

The mountainous areas are likely to be cooler and less humid. In autumn, the weather is pleasant throughout the state, while winters, especially in the mountains, are cold and snowy. It can snow more than 100 inches per year. That's more than 8 feet! Lake Erie keeps the northwest corner cooler. July tends to be the state's warmest month as temperatures are between 80 and 90 degrees Farenheit. January is the coldest month, with temperatures falling to about 23°F.

Pennsylvania's Wildlife

Pennsylvania's forests are home to trees such as maple, oak, birch, pine, and elm. In the fall, Pennsylvania forests and hills turn lovely shades of orange, red, and yellow as the leaves change colors. Flowers bloom alongside the trees. Pennsylvania's state flower, the mountain laurel, grows wild in the forests, as do azaleas and rhododendrons.

Pennsylvania's forests and fields are also home to rabbits, raccoons, opossums, deer, squirrels, and bats. The white-tailed deer can be found nearly everywhere and is the official state animal. On a nature hike, visitors might also spot beavers, minks, woodchucks, and chipmunks.

Snow blankets a covered bridge after a winter storm in Lancaster County.

History buffs of all ages will enjoy a visit to Philadelphia, the cradle of liberty in the United States. Visitors can start by viewing the Liberty Bell. Each year, more than one million people visit this symbol of American independence. Tourists can also see the room where members of the Continental Congress signed the Declaration of Independence. They can walk through the house where Betsy Ross may have sewn the first American flag. The National Constitution Center boasts one of the first printed copies of the US Constitution.

Exploring the Nation's Cradle of Liberty

At the Museum of the American Revolution, General George Washington's Headquarters Tent is on display. That tent traveled with him throughout the American Revolution. He made many of the war's most important decisions there.

Best of all, these landmarks sit within a few blocks of each other in downtown Philadelphia. To round out a perfect day of sightseeing, visitors can stroll to the nearby Reading Terminal Market. There they can browse the stalls of more than eighty merchants. Vendors offer fresh-baked **Amish** goods, local meat and poultry, ethnic foods, and much more. Many sightseers end their day with a long-time Philly favorite—a cheesesteak smothered in onions.

The Liberty Bell in Philadelphia draws more than a million tourists each year.

Black bears and bobcats were once almost extinct, but those species are making a comeback.

The state is also home to many different types of birds. There are plenty of wild turkeys and ruffed grouse. Ducks, geese, and herons can be found feeding at the state's waterways. Robins, sparrows, larks, chickadees, owls, hawks, and falcons may be seen in the skies or perched in the trees.

Saving Species

Many species—or types—of plants and animals that lived in the state hundreds or thousands of years ago are no longer around. This is mostly because of the changes humans made to the land when they settled in the region. Forests were cut down and waterways were rerouted, destroying the natural homes and food sources of many animals. Overhunting and pollution have also affected certain animal species. They have become endangered—that is, in danger of dying out or disappearing from the state.

Some species have been saved from becoming extinct (dying out). Bald eagles used to fly across Pennsylvania skies and nest in the tall trees. However, for most of the twentieth century (1900s), there were almost no bald eagles left in the state. Laws were passed restricting people from harming these eagles. Laws protecting the eagles meant that conservationists could breed these beautiful birds and release them back into the wild. As a result, the population slowly began to increase. Today, you might see bald eagles living in watery areas in most of the state's counties. Elk are another example. These animals have twice become almost extinct in the Allegheny Mountains. But today, Pennsylvania has several hundred elk.

Colorful leaves are among Pennsylvania's top attractions in the fall.

A number of species of plants and animals are still endangered in Pennsylvania. Among them are birds such as the short-eared owl, mammals such as the Delmarva fox squirrel, and some types of sturgeons, shiners, sunfish, and other fish.

Bald eagles have made a comeback in Pennsylvania after nearly becoming extinct.

Something for Everyone

Pennsylvania's geography offers something for everyone. With its mountains and hills, forests and fields, rivers and lakes, it is both beautiful and useful for the people who live there and its visitors.

What Lives in Pennsylvania?

Apples are a key crop across the state.

Pennsylvania is one of the country's biggest producers of Christmas trees.

Pennsylvania produces nearly half of all mushrooms grown in the United States.

Flora

Apples Pennsylvania ranks fourth among all states in apple production, according to the US Apple Association. Each year the state produces 400 to 500 million pounds (181 million to 227 million kg) of apples. The land in the state's south-central region is especially suited for growing apples, but apple orchards can be found across the state.

Christmas Trees Pennsylvania ranks among the nation's top-five states in Christmas tree production. The average growing time for a typical 6- to 7-foot (1.8 to 2.1 m) Christmas tree is seven years. Types of trees grown in Pennsylvania include the eastern white pine, balsam fir, and others.

Corn Large cornfields stretch across farmland in many areas of Pennsylvania. The state's farms produced more than 122 million bushels of corn in 2016. That makes Pennsylvania the largest corn-producing state along the Eastern Seaboard.

Grapes Pennsylvania is one of the top grape-producing states in the nation. These grapes are eaten fresh, canned, made into juice, and made into wine. In fact, Pennsylvania also ranks among the nation's top-ten wine-producing states.

Mushrooms Each year, more than fifty mushroom farms in Chester County in southeastern Pennsylvania produce about 400 million pounds (181 million kilograms) of mushrooms. That represents nearly half of total US mushroom production. The mushroom industry contributes an estimated $2.7 billion to the local economy and employs nearly ten thousand workers.

Fauna

Great Dane Pennsylvania named the Great Dane as its state dog in 1965. Why? Pennsylvania founder William Penn owned a Great Dane. In early Pennsylvania, colonists used the giant dogs to help them hunt.

Pennsylvania Firefly While fireflies are common in many places in the United States, only Pennsylvania has a species named after it. The *Photuris pennsylvanica* is also known as the lightning bug or glowworm. Each summer, Forest County in the northwestern part of the state holds a Firefly Festival in late June to enjoy the mating display of the fireflies.

The Pennsylvania firefly lights up the night during the summer months.

Rainbow Trout Sport fishing is popular in Pennsylvania, and trout are one of the most prized fish of all. Easily identified by the rainbow stripe down its side, the rainbow trout can be found in lakes and streams across the state. Rainbow trout typically grow to a length of 12 to 18 inches (30.5 to 45.7 cm).

Ruffed Grouse Pennsylvania named the ruffed grouse as its state bird in 1931. A medium-sized grouse, the ruffed grouse is commonly found in forests throughout Pennsylvania. Grouse hunting is a popular sport in the state.

Rainbow trout are colorful, fun to catch, and tasty when cooked.

White-Tailed Deer A medium-sized deer, white-tailed deer can be found across Pennsylvania. In 1959, the state named it the state animal. Swift and graceful, white-tailed deer can run more than 45 miles per hour (72 kilometers per hour).

This print, based on a painting by Benjamin West, shows William Penn meeting with Native Americans in Philadelphia.

2 The History of Pennsylvania

Pennsylvania earned its nickname as "The Keystone State" with good reason. A keystone is a stone at the center of an arch that locks the structure together and gives the other stones support. In colonial times, Pennsylvania was in the center of the other colonies and a center for buying, selling, and trading. In 1776, Philadelphia hosted the meetings that brought about the US Declaration of Independence. A decade later, the US Constitution was written there. Today, Pennsylvania remains an important state, both for economy and politics.

Early Settlers

The region that would become Pennsylvania played an important role in the history of European settlement of America. Many historians believe that English captain John Smith was the first European to visit the region. Smith is believed to have sailed up the Susquehanna River and met with the Susquehannock people in 1608.

A year later, the Dutch government hired Henry Hudson to sail to North America in search of a water route to Asia. Hudson sailed into Delaware Bay and claimed the surrounding

FAST FACT
William Penn, a **Quaker**, had faced bad treatment in England for his religious beliefs. He founded Pennsylvania with the idea of having a colony where people of all religions would be welcome. He called this idea his "Holy Experiment." Overall, his experiment succeeded. Pennsylvania was more tolerant of different religions than most colonies.

Dutch explorer Henry Hudson sailed into Delaware Bay in the early 1600s.

land for the Dutch. Other Dutch explorers soon came and set up trading posts there, but they did not build permanent settlements.

In 1638, explorers from Sweden arrived and claimed the region. They called the area Nya Sverige, which meant "New Sweden." Tinicum Island, in the Delaware River, was later named the capital of the Swedish territory. (Today the site is part of Pennsylvania. It is located southwest of present-day Philadelphia.) In 1654, the Swedes captured a Dutch fort in what is now Delaware, but the Swedish did not control the settlement for long. The following year, the Dutch took the settlement back for their government.

Then, in 1664, the English claimed the same area for the Duke of York. The English gained and maintained control of the region. Nearly twenty years later, the English king, Charles II, gave William Penn a portion of that land. This portion later became Pennsylvania.

William Penn's Charter

William Penn was a Quaker—a member of a religious group called the Society of Friends. The Quakers were not treated well in England, and Penn wanted to establish a new colony where Quakers—and others—could live peacefully and follow the religion they wanted. He asked King Charles II to grant him land west of the Delaware River for this purpose. The king agreed, both because he owed money to Penn's father and because he wanted to honor Penn's father, who was loyal to him. Charles II signed the land grant in 1681.

This grant, called the Charter of Pennsylvania, gave Penn the right to establish a colony in North America. The king named the colony Pennsylvania ("Penn's Woods"), in honor of William Penn's father.

Penn, as proprietor (governor), arrived in 1682. He and the other settlers organized the local government using a constitution that he called the Frame of Government. This document said that people had a right to own land and govern themselves. Many European countries at the time were ruled by kings and queens. Therefore, the idea of self-governing (the people ruling themselves without a king or queen) was new.

By the mid-1700s, Philadelphia was the largest city in the colonies.

Penn also helped plan the city of Philadelphia. He chose its name, which means "brotherly love" in Greek. The city was central to Pennsylvania society, and it grew to become the largest city in the American colonies.

Penn became very sick in 1712 and was no longer able to carry out his duties as proprietor of Pennsylvania. His wife, Hannah, took over and ran the colony until her death in 1726.

Spreading West

The population of Pennsylvania continued to grow, but most of the new settlers lived in what is now eastern Pennsylvania. Westward expansion was limited by the thick forests, the mountains, and a lack of roads wide enough for

The Native People

Native Americans lived in what is now Pennsylvania for thousands of years before the first Europeans arrived. The original groups include the Erie, Iroquois—especially the Seneca and the Oneida—the Lenape, the Munsee, the Shawnee, and the Susquehannock. They spoke Algonquian or Iroquoian languages. The Susquehannock, who lived along the Susquehanna River, were known as fierce warriors, and they traded animal hides and other goods for European supplies such as cloth and tools. The Lenape and Munsee, who considered themselves related, lived in the eastern part of the state, near the Delaware River. The Erie and the Iroquois lived along the New York border, and the Shawnee in the central and western parts of present-day Pennsylvania.

These groups moved with the seasons. In the summer, they might live near the rivers, where they could catch fish. In the fall, they might move toward the mountains, where they could eat wild berries, nuts, and other plants. The men did the hunting, and the women did the home chores and the farming, growing corn, beans, and squash. They wore animal-skin clothing, sometimes decorated with beads, and lived in wigwams made of poles covered with bark. Sometimes they protected their villages with palisades or log walls. They used dugout canoes to travel on the region's many rivers.

Despite the efforts of a few groups of European settlers, in particular the Quakers, to treat the Native Americans fairly, almost all of the original inhabitants of Pennsylvania were driven west in the 1700s, eventually being settled in Oklahoma. The Shawnee moved to Ohio after the American Revolution before being forced out. The Susquehannock were nearly wiped out by diseases, although the final group of twenty was massacred in 1763 by a mob.

Today, there are no federally recognized Native American nations in Pennsylvania. The

Many Native Americans in Pennsylvania lived in wigwams.

Lenape entered a union with the Cherokee in Oklahoma and didn't regain their independent status until 1996. There are about sixteen thousand surviving Lenape, with a few living in communities in New Jersey and Pennsylvania.

Spotlight on the Lenape

The Lenape nation has called the region of Pennsylvania home for over ten thousand years.

Clans: The Lenape were divided into three clans, known as Wolf, Turtle, and Turkey. Families were important to the Lenape way of life. Lenape communities could vary in size from small groups of twenty-five to thirty people to large villages of two hundred people.

Homes: Many Lenape families lived in wigwams, round houses built with wood branches and covered with bark or animal hide. Some lived in longhouses, a rectangular structure that usually had a high roof and no windows.

Entertainment: Men and boys played lacrosse, while both boys and girls played a game in which a ball was kicked. Men and women contributed to storytelling, art, and music.

Clothing: Much of the clothing worn by the Lenape was made from animal hides. Men wore breechcloths, also known as loincloths, moccasins, and animal-skin robes in the winter. Women wore similar robes with knee-length skirts, and sometimes jewelry made of animal bone or shell. The women carried their babies on their backs in cradleboards.

Art: The Lenape are known for their beadwork and basketmaking. They also crafted wampum, beads made out of shells. The designs on beadwork or wampum often told a story.

horse-drawn wagons. However, some **settlers** did venture west in search of more land.

Both France and Britain wanted **control of** the land west of the established colonies, in spite of the fact that the area was already inhabited by Native Americans. French and British newcomers started settlements in the western lands. Both countries built military forts in the region. This included land that is now part of **western** Pennsylvania. From 1689 to 1763, France **and** Britain fought four different wars over **land.**

Some Native American groups took **sides** with one country or the other. In 1754, the French and Indian War—the last of the **four** wars—broke out. One of the first battles of this war was fought at Fort Necessity, near Farmington in southwestern **Pennsylvania.** There, the French and their Native allies defeated George Washington's army. It **was** the only time in his military career that Washington surrendered to an enemy. **The site** is now Fort Necessity National Battlefield.

The French and Indian War lasted **nine** years. In the end, Britain won. As a result of the 1763 treaty ending the war, the British controlled land in Canada, a large amount of land between the colonies and the **Mississippi** River, and some land in what is now Florida.

George Washington saw his first military action in the French and Indian War.

Forming a New Nation

By the mid-1700s, many colonists were unhappy with British control. They did not like Britain's taxes and trade rules. Many wanted the colonies to become independent and govern **themselves.** In 1774, representatives from most of the American colonies met in Philadelphia for **the** First Continental Congress. They decided that the colonies would no longer trade with Britain.

By April 1775, the American **Revolution** had begun, and colonists were fighting **the** British. A month after the start of the **war,** the Second Continental Congress began meeting in Philadelphia. The following **year,** it voted for independence from Britain **and** issued the Declaration of Independence. The Declaration of Independence stated **that** since Britain had denied the colonies **their** rights, the colonies were declaring **themselves** independent and no longer tied to **Britain.**

Though colonial forces won some **battles** at the beginning of the war, the colonists' Continental Army faced many problems fighting the British. The British military men **were** well trained and had spent years fighting **in** or preparing to fight in battles. Most **colonial** soldiers were craftsmen or farmers or had held other nonmilitary jobs. Fighting and traveling from battle to battle was new to them. At first, these colonists did not have good weapons or the skills to use them. Over time, they grew

Colonial leaders signed the Declaration of Independence in Philadelphia in 1776.

Famous Pennsylvanians

Marian Anderson

Daniel Boone

Marian Anderson

Born in 1897 in Philadelphia, Anderson was one of the most talented singers of the twentieth century. In 1955, she became the first African American singer to perform as a member of New York City's famous Metropolitan Opera. She performed at President John F. Kennedy's inauguration in 1961. Her success helped pave the way for other African American singers.

Daniel Boone

Born in Berks County in 1734, Boone became one of America's most famous frontiersmen. He blazed the Wilderness Road across the Appalachian Mountains and founded the settlement of Boonesborough in Kentucky. The trail he opened soon carried thousands of settlers into new lands.

James Buchanan

The only US president to come from Pennsylvania, Buchanan served from 1857 to 1861. Serving in the years just prior to the Civil War, he hoped for compromise between the Northern and Southern states but failed to bring it about. He is the only president to have been a lifelong bachelor.

Andrew Carnegie

Born in Scotland, Carnegie came to Pittsburgh with his family when he was young. As an adult, he founded the Carnegie Steel Company. He later sold the company for nearly $500 million. He devoted the later years of his life to giving away most of his fortune. Carnegie established thousands of libraries. He also founded Carnegie Technical Schools, which merged with the Mellon Institute in 1967 to become Carnegie Mellon University.

Benjamin Franklin

Best-selling author. Printer. Inventor. Statesman. Franklin did it all. As an author and publisher, his yearly *Poor Richard's Almanack* appeared for more than twenty-five years. His inventions included the lightning rod and bifocal glasses. He signed both the Declaration of Independence and the US Constitution.

Milton Hershey

Kisses, Mounds, and Reese's are just a few of the brands that are part of the chocolate empire Milton Hershey began in 1894. The entire town of Hershey grew up around the business. Hershey gave much of his wealth to worthy causes, such as the Milton Hershey School, which enrolls two thousand students today. In 2017, the Hersheypark theme park drew more than three million visitors.

Milton Hershey

Billie Holliday

A noted African American jazz singer whose career spanned more than twenty-five years, Holliday influenced jazz and pop music for decades. She recorded a number of successful songs and albums in the 1930s and 1940s. She died in 1959 at the age of forty-four, but she was honored with a Grammy Lifetime Achievement Award in 1987.

Betsy Ross

According to legend, Ross sewed the first American flag at her home in Philadelphia in 1776 after meeting with General George Washington to discuss the design. No one knows for sure if the legend is true, but we do know that she was a well-known seamstress and successful businesswoman.

Betsy Ross

stronger and more skilled, but battles **against** the British were still very difficult to win.

A few major battles in the American Revolution occurred in Pennsylvania. In September 1777, General George **Washington** and his men fought British troops at the Battle of Brandywine. Washington's men were forced to retreat. Later that month, the British defeated a colonial army in the Battle of Paoli near Philadelphia, and a few days after that, the British took over the city. Washington's forces again faced British troops near Philadelphia at the Battle of Germantown in October. The British won the battle, and the colonial army had to retreat.

The following winter months were difficult for many colonial troops. Starting in mid-December, Washington and his men **stayed in** Valley Forge, located northwest of **Philadelphia**. His army was cold, tired, and hungry. The men did not have enough warm clothing, blankets, or food. During the winter at **Valley** Forge, many soldiers died from illness. **Others** deserted—or ran away from—the army.

Washington's troops faced a rough winter in Valley Forge.

In February 1778, conditions began to improve. More supplies were brought in. **Baron** Friedrich von Steuben, a military man **from** Prussia (an area largely in the present-day country of Germany), volunteered to help **train** Washington's men. By spring of that year, they had regained their strength and confidence, and they continued to fight British forces. With help from France, the colonial **armies** began to win some battles against the **British**. The British forces left Philadelphia in **June**.

As the fighting continued, the British found allies among some Native American groups. In July 1778, some Iroquois in the region joined with the British to fight **groups** of settlers living in northeastern Pennsylvania. The area, known as the Wyoming Valley, is near present-day Wilkes-Barre. A few **hundred** colonial troops and settlers were killed during the Wyoming Valley Massacre, and many settlers fled. In turn, colonial forces later destroyed several Iroquois villages in the area.

Pennsylvania did make one important contribution to the war effort. The **Pennsylvania** Long Rifle was developed in the early 1700s. Historians credit Martin Meylin, who came to Lancaster County from Germany, with inventing this gun. The gun barrel was longer than those on the muskets used by the British forces. It was also rifled, which means there were spiral grooves inside the barrel that gave spin to the bullet. This spin makes the bullet **fly** straighter and makes the gun more accurate.

The gun could shoot five times farther than the British muskets. Its range was about 300 yards (274 meters), and it was very **accurate**. Use of the Long Rifle allowed soldiers from the colonial army to hide in wooded areas and hit enemy targets while staying out of range of the British guns. This tactic helped win the First Battle of Saratoga in 1777, **which** was one of the turning points of the **war**.

The American Revolution **officially** ended in 1783, and the colonies **became** an independent nation, the United **States** of America. From May to September of 1787, the Constitutional Convention **met** in Philadelphia. After much debate **within** the Convention, a national constitution was written. Then the colonies began to ratify, or approve, the document. Pennsylvania was the second state (after Delaware) to approve the Constitution, doing so on December 12, 1787. Philadelphia served as the capital of the new nation from 1790 to 1800, when the national government moved to Washington, DC.

A meeting in Philadelphia in 1787 led to the drafting of the US Constitution.

FAST FACT

Pennsylvania served as home to three US capitals during the American Revolution against England: Philadelphia, Lancaster, and York. When the British captured Philadelphia, the government moved to Lancaster for a single day. Then they retreated even farther west to York. After the war, Philadelphia also served as the US capital between 1790 and 1800.

Continued Growth in the 1800s

Canal boats carried coal from the mines to cities during the 1800s.

Pennsylvania continued to grow and be successful into the 1800s. Cities flourished, farms thrived, and industry expanded. Pennsylvania manufactured a large portion of the country's goods. Its steel mills, coal mines, and factories helped the economy. Pennsylvania was also well known for its glass production.

In 1825, the Schuylkill Canal became the first long canal project in Pennsylvania. It was made up of many separate canals and dam-created pools. By 1828, it measured 108 miles (174 km) in length, stretching from Port Carbon via Reading to Philadelphia. The Schuylkill Canal was used mainly to carry coal. In 1834, the Pennsylvania Canal was opened. It included a railroad segment that went up one side of the mountains and down the other, which enabled people and goods to more easily cross the Alleghenies. Although a series of large floods eventually destroyed many of the canals, a few stretches of the Pennsylvania Canal have been preserved or restored. During the 1850s, railroads were expanded throughout the state, further improving Pennsylvania's transportation system.

Pennsylvania chartered Penn State University in 1855. It was one of the country's first colleges set up to use science to improve farming. It was built on 200 acres (81 ha) donated by James Irvin of Bellefonte.

Founding president Evan Pugh and others urged Congress to pass the Morrill Land-Grant Act in 1862. This act allowed states to sell land given to them by the federal government and to use the money they received to pay for colleges. Penn State is Pennsylvania's only land-grant university.

Slavery and the Civil War

In colonial times, many Pennsylvanians enslaved African Americans. Slavery gradually disappeared in Pennsylvania after a law against it was adopted in 1780. The state became one of the many safe places for free Black people or fugitives from slavery to start new lives. The Underground Railroad was a network of people who helped enslaved African Americans from the South escape to freedom in the North and in Canada, where slavery was illegal. Some historians estimate that more than one hundred thousand people tried to leave the South through the Underground Railroad. Many fugitives from slavery died along the way. Others were caught and enslaved again. However, many managed to make their way to freedom. The borough (town) of Columbia, on the Susquehanna River in Lancaster County, became a popular place for people who had freed themselves from slavery to settle.

A piece of the Underground Railroad was discovered in Columbia. Stone bridge piers and part of a lock on the Pennsylvania Canal were partially uncovered. According to the National Underground Railroad Network to Freedom (run by the National Park Service), these structures were used to help enslaved people escape to freedom.

One of the giants of the Underground Railroad was Daniel Hughes, and he was a very large man indeed. He was at least 6 feet, 7 inches (2 meters) tall and weighed about 300 pounds (136 kg). He moved north of Williamsport in 1828 to an area that has since been renamed Freedom Road and worked moving lumber on a river raft. He operated on the Susquehanna River between Williamsport and an area just north of Baltimore, Maryland.

Established in 1855, Pennsylvania State University is the state's largest university.

This Pennsylvania house was a stop on the Underground Railroad.

Union states without slavery
Union States with slavery
Confederate States
Territories

This map shows the breakdown of Union and Confederate states during the Civil War.

This job gave him the ability to smuggle enslaved people from Maryland, where slavery was allowed, to central Pennsylvania.

Hughes would bring people escaping from slavery up the river and hide them in a house in a wooded area or in caves on or near his property. His wife and sixteen children would sneak food to the escapees before taking them to Trout Run for the next stop on the railroad in Elmira, New York. They were often helped by the wealthy of Williamsport or by people from local churches, mostly Quakers. The system was very effective. Not one person helped by Hughes was ever caught.

Slavery was one of the reasons the Civil War began in 1861. A total of eleven Southern states seceded—or separated—from the United States. They formed the Confederate States of America. Pennsylvania remained a part of the United States, which was also called the Union. The state sent more than four hundred thousand men to fight the Confederate forces. State residents provided supplies and food for the Union troops. Pennsylvania also produced much of the military equipment that was used.

Confederate and Union forces fought many bloody battles. One of the most famous was fought in Gettysburg, Pennsylvania, in 1863. The Battle of Gettysburg lasted from July 1 through July 3. About fifty thousand soldiers were wounded or killed, making the battle one of the bloodiest in US history. Gettysburg marked the northernmost point that any Confederate army reached. The Confederates were defeated there and forced to retreat. President Abraham Lincoln delivered his famous Gettysburg Address on the battlefield in November 1863. This short but powerful speech honored those who had fought and died for the country and its freedoms.

The South eventually surrendered to the North in 1865, and the war ended. The Confederate states rejoined the United States, the Thirteenth **Amendment** to the US Constitution ended slavery nationwide, and the country started rebuilding and reuniting.

The Union victory at the Battle of Gettysburg helped to turn the tide of the Civil War.

Industry in the 1800s

Through the end of the 1800s, Pennsylvania's economy continued to thrive. In addition to mining, manufacturing, and farming, there was new industry. Oil had been found in the northwestern corner of the state, and its discovery was the beginning of the American oil industry. Jobs were plentiful, and people from the war-torn Southern states, as well as

FAST FACT

In the 1800s and 1900s, Pennsylvania was the "steel capital of the world." Giant companies such as US Steel and Bethlehem Steel employed thousands of workers. Steel manufactured in Pennsylvania built such famous structures as the Brooklyn Bridge and the Empire State Building.

Make Your Own Embossed Metal Artwork

For decades, much of Pennsylvania's economy revolved around steel production. This activity uses a soft, pliable metal called ArtEmboss and colored pencils to create an art project. It involves making a pattern in the metal and then painting or coloring it in. Historically, this type of art was found across Mexico and South America, as well as in Ireland and Scotland.

Supplies:

- ArtEmboss sheets
- Colored pencils
- Paper

Directions:

1. Sketch a pattern on a sheet of paper corresponding to the size of your piece of metal. Start with a fairly simple pattern.
2. Place a magazine or stack of newspapers under the piece of metal.
3. Following your pattern, emboss your design in the metal from the back, using a soft pencil.
4. Turn the drawing over.
5. Use colored pencils to fill in the spaces between the lines in your pattern. The lines you embossed will remain raised, while the colored areas will remain lower.

immigrants from Scotland, Ireland, Russia, and Eastern Europe, came to Pennsylvania in hopes of making better lives. Work in the factories and mines, however, proved dangerous and did not provide as much money as the workers had expected. In the late 1800s, many of these workers demanded better pay and safer working conditions. Some of the first American labor unions were formed in Pennsylvania. These were groups of workers who joined together to demand better conditions and better pay.

These boys worked at a Pennsylvania coal mine in the late 1800s.

The Twentieth Century to the Present

In the early twentieth century, Pennsylvania was still one of the leading industrial states. Then the Great Depression, which began in 1929, caused massive unemployment and hardship throughout the country. Like many other states, Pennsylvania was hit hard. At one point, almost 80 percent of the workers at the state's steel mills and in its coal mines had lost their jobs. Since steel mills and coal mines were two of the biggest industries in Pennsylvania, many people living in the state were unemployed. Without jobs, these workers had no money to feed their families or keep their homes. Most people could not afford to buy many products, so the merchants and farmers who provided these products to the public also suffered. Many people left the state to search for work elsewhere.

The state and national governments set up programs to help. Workers were employed by the government to build and fix bridges, highways, and dams. Others were paid to work in the forests.

In 1939, World War II began in Europe. The United States joined the war in 1941. As

Pennsylvania supplied many troops during World War II.

in World War I, in which the United States fought from 1917 to 1918, the state sent many soldiers to serve in the military. Pennsylvania mines and factories also provided supplies for the war effort. Workers were hired to operate the steel mills, factories, and coal mines.

After the war, the state's economy improved for a time, but then demand for Pennsylvania steel and coal declined, and many factories were shut down. It took many years, but the state's economy eventually bounced back.

One improvement occurred in 1973. The Harley-Davidson motorcycle assembly operation, which had built nearly ninety thousand motorcycles for the United States military during World War II, was moved to York, Pennsylvania. The company opened a museum in York, which includes a Kids Corner. The museum allows visitors to learn how these vehicles are made.

Mining and manufacturing continued, but other areas of the economy, such as services, became more significant. New industries became important, including the computer industry. Pennsylvania played an important early role in the development of computers. ENIAC, the first large-scale general-purpose electronic digital computer, was built in Philadelphia at the University of Pennsylvania in 1946. The Remington Rand Corporation, also in Philadelphia, made the first commercial computer, the UNIVAC I, in 1951.

That first computer was delivered to the US Census Bureau, a government agency that keeps a count of every person who lives in the United States. In 1952, a UNIVAC was used by CBS News to accurately predict who would win the presidential election that year. The company became Sperry-Rand in 1955 and was later renamed Unisys. Located in Blue

Bell, the company sells billions of dollars' worth of technology goods and services.

Because the state had relied for so **many years** on the mining and manufacturing industries, Pennsylvania's environment suffered. Air and water pollution from factories and coal mining became serious problems. This was especially true in Pittsburgh, where a lot of steel was made. However, in recent decades, the state's air and water have generally become cleaner. This was partly a result of changes in the state's **economy.** New state and federal laws protecting the environment were another important factor.

Early computers, such as this UNIVAC I, were much larger than today's computers.

Gerrymandering

Aside from protecting the environment, another key recent issue in Pennsylvania relates to politics. Every vote counts in an election. However, in some states, **elections** are complicated by gerrymandering. Gerrymandering involves moving the boundaries of an area of voters to give an advantage to **one** political party or another. In the 2018 **election** year, gerrymandering was an important **issue** in many states, including Pennsylvania.

In Pennsylvania, the state supreme **court** drew a new map for the state's eighteen US congressional districts. The previous map gave an advantage to Republicans, who usually won more than two-thirds of the seats in Congress, even though there are more registered Democratic voters in the state than Republicans. The new map was designed to create fair races in more districts.

In the past, the state legislators had created the map for the governor's signature or **veto.** In 2018, however, the state supreme court told the Republican-controlled legislature **and**

The Mummers Parade: Ringing in the New Year

A Philadelphia tradition since 1901, the Mummers Parade rings in the New Year in style each January 1. From early morning through late afternoon, dozens of string bands dance and strut their way through Center City, performing a wide variety of music. Dressed in lavish costumes that often featured glitter, sequins, and feathers, more than twenty thousand mummers participated in the parade in 2018.

The concept of mummers dates back to early Egypt, pagan Rome and Greece, and several European countries. Today, bands work all year on their costumes and routines. They compete for prizes in five main divisions, as well as a number of subdivisions. The string bands play, and often compose, their own music, while the other divisions mostly march to recorded music.

More than one hundred thousand spectators lined the parade route in 2018. Mummers march even through wind and cold. Since 1901, the parade has been canceled only twice (due to non-weather issues) and postponed only twenty-two times. The parade is always a crowd pleaser. In 2017, *USA Today*'s Reader's Choice survey named it as America's top holiday parade.

The Mummers Parade has been a Pennsylvania tradition for more than one hundred years.

Democratic governor to agree on a **redrawn map** and gave them a deadline. When **they** couldn't agree within a certain time **frame, the** court stepped in to create its own **map.**

Pennsylvania Republicans strongly disagreed with the court's action. They asked the US Supreme Court to **intervene.** Justice Samuel Alito refused to overturn the state supreme court's action, because the US Supreme Court usually does not get involved in cases with state constitutional issues.

Will Pennsylvania's new districts actually **make** the state's elections fairer and more competitive? Will the change make the balance of power in the state more even? Only time will tell.

Philadelphia, like
Pennsylvania as a whole,
is home to people of all
different backgrounds.

3 Who Lives in Pennsylvania?

ennsylvania's population of nearly thirteen million people includes people of all **ethnicities**. Non-Hispanic whites represent 76.5 percent of the population, according to 2017 US Census Bureau data. African Americans are the next largest group, accounting for 11.9 percent, followed by Hispanics at 7.3 percent and **Asians** at 3.6 percent. The state's population also includes American Indians, Native Hawaiians and other Pacific Islanders, and 2 percent who identify as belonging to two or more races.

In 1790, when the first census, or count, of all the people in the United States was taken, the population of Pennsylvania was almost 435,000. Sixty years later, the number of people living in Pennsylvania had dramatically increased to more than two million. The number of **residents** continued to grow rapidly. But long before settlers arrived in Pennsylvania, thousands of Native Americans called the region their **home**.

Native Americans

Native Americans hunted, farmed, and lived for centuries on the land that is now **Pennsylvania**. Major groups in the region when the first

FAST FACT

Surprisingly, the people referred to as Pennsylvania Dutch aren't Dutch at all. "Pennsylvania Dutch" actually refers to the German settlers who came to the Lancaster County area of Pennsylvania in the seventeenth and eighteenth centuries. They were known as "Deutsch," the German word for "German." The term also refers to a German dialect spoken in Amish communities.

A dancer at a powwow in Pennsylvania keeps Native American traditions alive.

Europeans arrived included the Iroquois, Susquehannock, Shawnee, and Lenape. Loss of land and hunting grounds, European settlement, and diseases brought by the Europeans decreased the population of indigenous people in the region.

The US Census Bureau estimated that in 2017, Native Americans made up only about 0.4 percent of the state's population. Today, there are no federally recognized Native American reservations in Pennsylvania. However, many Native Americans from different nations live in the state. Native Americans in Pennsylvania own farms, have jobs in towns and cities, and hold office in local and state governments. Throughout the year, festivals and powwows (Native American cultural celebrations, with dancing and more) take place across the state. Pennsylvania also has many historical landmarks and museums dedicated to indigenous people.

The Pennsylvania Dutch

The ancestors of the people known as the Pennsylvania Dutch began coming to Pennsylvania in the seventeenth century. Many wanted to get away from wars in Europe and find religious freedom in a new land. By 1775, the Pennsylvania Dutch made up one-third of the colony's population. Today, most of the Pennsylvania Dutch live in the Lancaster area. There are close to one hundred thousand people

Notable foods that are identified with Pennsylvania include cheesesteaks, pierogies, shoofly pie, scrapple, and soft pretzels. Soft pretzels are not only tasty but also easy to make. Here's one simple recipe.

Make Your Own Soft Pretzels

Ingredients

- 4 teaspoons active dry yeast
- 1 teaspoon sugar
- 1¼ cups warm water
- 5 cups all-purpose flour
- ½ cup white sugar
- 1½ teaspoons salt
- 1 tablespoon vegetable oil
- ½ cup baking soda
- 4 cups hot water
- ¼ cup salt for the topping

Directions

1. Dissolve yeast and 1 teaspoon sugar in 1¼ cups warm water in a small bowl and let stand until creamy.
2. In a larger bowl, mix flour, ½ cup sugar, and salt.
3. Make a well in the center. Then add the vegetable oil and the yeast mixture.
4. Mix this all together, adding more water if the mixture seems dry.
5. Knead the dough until it's smooth.
6. Next, lightly oil a large bowl. Place the dough inside and turn it until it is coated.
7. Cover it with plastic wrap and let it sit in a warm place until it rises to about double its size.
8. Preheat your oven to 450°F (230°C).
9. Lightly grease two baking sheets.
10. Dissolve baking soda in 4 cups of hot water.
11. Place your dough on a lightly floured surface and divide it into 12 equal pieces.
12. Roll and stretch each piece into a rope and then twist it into a pretzel shape.
13. Dip each pretzel into the baking soda solution and place the pretzels onto the baking sheets.
14. Top them with salt.
15. Bake for about 8 minutes until browned.
16. Enjoy your soft pretzel treat!

Amish buggies are a common sight in Lancaster County.

FAST FACT

Seating 106,572, Beaver Stadium at Pennsylvania State University has the second-highest capacity of any college football stadium in the United States. In addition, Penn State's Berkey Creamery is the largest university creamery in the world. Ice cream gurus Ben Cohen and Jerry Greenfield (founders of Ben and Jerry's) took a course on ice cream making there.

in the area with Pennsylvania Dutch ancestry. Many of them belong to such Christian branches as the Amish, Mennonites, and Brethren.

Some Pennsylvania Dutch live in much the same way as their ancestors. They do not believe in modern conveniences such as electricity or cars. They run their farms in nearly the same manner as their ancestors did centuries ago. On some roads in Lancaster County, Pennsylvania Dutch horse-drawn carriages can be seen alongside cars. However, not all Pennsylvania Dutch live that way. Some people of Pennsylvania Dutch descent use all types of modern technology and conveniences.

Lancaster County in southeastern Pennsylvania is home to the second-largest population of Amish people in the world. (Only the Holmes County area in Ohio has more Amish.) In Lancaster County and in some other parts of the state, people can visit museums and historic farmhouses that share the history and culture of the Pennsylvania Dutch.

A Diverse Population

According to the US Census Bureau, as of 2017, Pennsylvania's population was about 76.5 percent white. Some are descended from the earliest European settlers: the Dutch, the Swedish, and the English. Other white residents can trace their ancestors to the German, Polish, Italian, Irish, Scottish, and other immigrants who came to the state over the centuries. New European immigrants, as well as **Americans** with **European** backgrounds who relocate from other states, continue to move to Pennsylvania and make it their home.

Today, African Americans make up the largest minority group in the state. Slightly more than one-tenth of the population is African American. Between 1780 and 1847, **slavery** was gradually ended in Pennsylvania. **Many** formerly enslaved people chose to live in **and** around Philadelphia and other **Pennsylvania** cities, and many of their descendants make Pennsylvania their home today. Many **African** Americans from the South also settled in the state in the twentieth century. This was especially true in the years after World Wars I and II. Many factory and other industrial jobs were available in Pennsylvania at that time, and workers **in** these jobs tended to earn more money **than** people who worked on farms in the South.

A group of African American men in Philadelphia, 1864

Hispanic and Asian Pennsylvanians

More than nine hundred thousand Hispanic people live in Pennsylvania. Hispanics started moving to the state in the nineteenth century. Some came as experienced farmers and found work in agriculture. Others found jobs in different lines of work, and many opened their

Celebrities from Pennsylvania

Kevin Bacon

Philadelphia native Kevin Bacon has appeared in dozens of films, including *Footloose*, *JFK*, *Apollo 13*, and *A Few Good Men*.

Joe Biden

Born in Scranton, Biden served as the nation's vice president from 2009 to 2017. He also served as a US senator for Delaware for thirty-six years.

Guion Bluford

In 1983, Guion Bluford, a Philadelphia native, became the first African American astronaut to travel in space, as a crew member aboard the space shuttle *Challenger*.

Kobe Bryant

During a twenty-year career with the Los Angeles Lakers, Bryant won five NBA championships. He was an All-Star eighteen times and ranks third on the league's all-time regular season scoring list. Bryant was born in Philadelphia.

Bradley Cooper

Bradley Cooper is a versatile actor and director. He has received Academy Award nominations for his roles in *Silver Linings Playbook*, *American Hustle*, and *American Sniper*. Cooper was born in Philadelphia.

Joe Biden

Guion Bluford

Mark Cuban

Born in Pittsburgh, billionaire businessman Mark Cuban owns the NBA's Dallas Mavericks. He also is a star of the reality television series *Shark Tank*.

Eve

Philadelphia-born rapper Eve is a Grammy Award winner. She also has starred in films such as *Barbershop* and served as cohost on the talk show *The Talk*.

Tina Fey

Tina Fey is an actress and comedian known for her work on *Saturday Night Live* and *30 Rock*. She has also starred in films such as *Sisters* and *Date Night*. Fey was born in Upper Darby.

Tina Fey

Will Smith

Will Smith is a television and movie actor known for films such as *I Am Legend* and *Men in Black*. As a songwriter and rapper, he has won four Grammy Awards. Smith was born in Philadelphia.

Taylor Swift

One of the world's most popular recording artists, as of 2018 Swift had won ten Grammy Awards, ten Country Music Association Awards, and many other honors. Swift was born in Reading.

Taylor Swift

Philadelphia's Chinatown features many shops and restaurants.

own businesses. Many came from Puerto Rico, which is part of the United States. In recent years, the Hispanic population has grown rapidly to include people from Mexico, Cuba, the Dominican Republic, and other countries. In many of Pennsylvania's cities, you can find businesses, restaurants, and stores owned by Hispanic Americans. Throughout the year in different parts of Pennsylvania, residents hold festivals and other events celebrating Hispanic culture.

Asian Americans make up 3.6 percent of the state's population. The state's Asian population includes people of Indian, Chinese, Filipino, Vietnamese, Korean, and Japanese heritage. Some of these people are the children or grandchildren of immigrants who came to the state many years ago. Others are new residents. Regardless of how long they have lived in the state, their influence can be seen in different parts of Pennsylvania.

Philadelphia has a thriving Chinatown. This part of the city first attracted Chinese immigrants who arrived more than one hundred years ago. Visitors and residents have long enjoyed—and continue to enjoy—Chinatown's shops, restaurants, and cultural celebrations.

Constant Change

Some of Pennsylvania's best-known traditions were started by immigrants to celebrate their heritage. Philadelphia's highly popular Mummers Parade is one example. In addition, Pennsylvanians of different backgrounds enjoy

FAST FACT
Chinese New Year is based on the traditional Chinese calendar, which revolves around lunar patterns. Their New Year celebration varies from year to year. It falls sometime between late January and late February. In Philadelphia, the celebration features parades, dances, and food events.

Penn State University

Pennsylvania's Biggest Colleges and Universities

(Enrollment numbers are from *US News and World Report* 2019 college rankings.)

1. Pennsylvania State University, University Park
(40,835 undergraduate students)

2. Temple University, Philadelphia
(29,550 undergraduate students)

Temple University

3. University of Pittsburgh
(19,326 undergraduate students)

4. West Chester University
(14,451 undergraduate students)

5. Drexel University, Philadelphia
(13,272 undergraduate students)

6. Indiana University of Pennsylvania
(10,143 undergraduate students)

7. University of Pennsylvania, Philadelphia
(10,033 undergraduate students)

Bloomsburg University

8. Bloomsburg University
(8,606 undergraduate students)

9. Slippery Rock University
(7,638 undergraduate students)

10. Kutztown University
(7,489 undergraduate students)

Drexel University

A True Melting Pot

Pennsylvania's factories and mines employed thousands of immigrants in the 1800s.

From its earliest days as a colony, Pennsylvania has been a true melting pot for people from all around the world. The Dutch and the Swedes were the first to settle the area in the 1600s, followed by the English. When William Penn offered religious freedom in his new colony, people from across Europe streamed in. These included many Quakers from England, who came to escape persecution because of their religious beliefs.

The next big wave of immigrants brought people from across Europe. In particular, thousands of Germans arrived. Many settled in the rich farmlands of Lancaster County and surrounding areas. They brought with them their German language and culture. They represented many different religious groups, such as the Mennonites and the Amish. Today, many of the Amish still live and farm in the Lancaster area.

Between 1800 and 1860, Pennsylvania's population grew from 600,000 to 2.9 million. Many were immigrants coming to work in the transportation and coal industries. This wave of immigrants included many Irish. Later in the 1800s, the growing steel industry drew a new wave of immigrants. Many were from central, southern, and eastern European countries such as Italy, Croatia, Germany, Russia, and Poland.

At the beginning of the twentieth century, the wave of immigrants from central, southern, and eastern Europe continued. During the first half of the twentieth century, tens of thousands of African Americans migrated from the South to Philadelphia in search of jobs. They formed one of the largest African American communities in a Northern city.

Over time, the pattern changed. In recent decades, the majority of Pennsylvania's immigrants have come from Asia and Latin America. Currently, the top countries immigrants come from are India, China, Mexico, the Dominican Republic, and Vietnam. In 2017, immigrants made up more than 6 percent of all Pennsylvania residents, while another 8 percent are native-born US citizens who have at least one immigrant parent.

celebrating their heritage. Irish **Americans and** others turn out for the annual Saint **Patrick's** Day parades in Philadelphia, Pittsburgh, Scranton, and other cities around the state. Philadelphia's Columbus Day parade honors **the** area's Italian Americans. An annual Polish **American** festival is held at the National Shrine of Our Lady of Czestochowa in Doylestown.

From its earliest days, people from many countries and cultures have made their homes in Pennsylvania. That is still true today. Just as in colonial times, Pennsylvania **remains** a true melting pot. The many different ethnicities and cultures of **Pennsylvanians** **bring** a rich **diversity** to the **state.**

This Saint Patrick's Day parade in Scranton celebrates Irish heritage.

Steelworkers have played
an important part in
Pennsylvania's economy.

4 At Work in Pennsylvania

In colonial days, Philadelphia served as a center for trade, while most people outside of the city made their living from farming. In the 1800s, the state moved to an industrial economy based on coal and steel. That continued into the mid-twentieth century. As the twentieth century ended and the twenty-first century began, the state once again had to find new ways to build its economy. Today, Pennsylvania has become home to a variety of tech-based businesses.

The agriculture, mining, manufacturing, and service industries help keep Pennsylvania's economy running. They supply goods and services used around the world, and they provide jobs for millions of people in Pennsylvania.

FAST FACT

Computer scientist Scott Fahlman of Carnegie Mellon University created the first smiley face emoticon back in the 1980s. Today, there are thousands of different emoticons, but smileys (and variations of them) remain extremely popular.

Agriculture

Agriculture and other industries that rely on natural resources have always played a large part in Pennsylvania's economy. The lumber industry was important during the eighteenth and nineteenth centuries. Millions of trees were harvested for lumber and for papermaking. As a result, Pennsylvania lost

Pennsylvania has a thriving lumber industry, including growing Christmas trees.

Longhorn cattle graze in a Lancaster County field.

most of its forests. Today, much of the state is again covered by trees, and the forest-products industry again plays an important role.

Instead of the pine and hemlock trees that once covered the land, hardwoods such as black cherry, oak, maple, walnut, poplar, and ash are now common. Pennsylvania produces about one-tenth of all the hardwood in the US, more than any other state. Pennsylvania also has many Christmas tree farms, which grow pine trees for the holidays.

Unlike the lumber industry, Pennsylvania's farming industry has remained steady, although in recent years less land has been devoted to farming. Today, about one-fourth of Pennsylvania is farmland. Pennsylvania farmers harvest wheat, oats, mushrooms, soybeans, potatoes, and corn. Many acres are dedicated to apple orchards. Farmers in the southern part of the state grow tomatoes, grapes, peaches, and strawberries. Pennsylvania also produces cut flowers, shrubs, and decorative trees for use across the country.

Animals raised in the state include hogs, sheep, and poultry. On many eastern and southeastern Pennsylvania fields, you might find herds of beef cattle grazing. Cows are also important to the dairy industry. Some Pennsylvania farmers raise llamas. Their hair can be used for clothing, and they can be trained to guard sheep herds.

Mining Remains Important

Mined products include limestone, used for cement and other construction products. Many construction companies also use sand and gravel from the state. Pennsylvania coal is used for processing iron ore, heating homes, and generating electricity at power plants.

Coal is still one of Pennsylvania's most important products, but mining can cause problems for the environment. A fire broke out in 1962 in abandoned coal mines under Centralia, in the eastern part of the state. Efforts to put out the fire failed. The worst mine fire in the United States was still burning more than fifty years later, and almost all of the town's residents had left.

In 1859, the first US oil well was dug in Titusville. Small amounts of oil are still produced in the western part of the state. The mining of natural gas by hydraulic fracturing, or fracking, is an important source of revenue for Pennsylvania as well. Fracking is a controversial method of mining because of its impact on the environment.

The Centralia mine fire that started in 1962 is still burning today.

Making Things

Andrew Carnegie came to the United States from Scotland with his family in the 1840s, when he was twelve, and the family settled in the Pittsburgh area. As a young man, Carnegie worked for the Pennsylvania Railroad, where he was promoted to increasingly important positions. He also invested money in other industrial companies.

Oil refining remains a major industry in Pennsylvania.

In the 1870s and 1880s, he started and purchased several steel mills, which he combined into the Carnegie Steel Company. The US needed more and more steel for buildings and industrial equipment. Carnegie Steel became one of the largest steel manufacturers in the country, and Andrew Carnegie became one of the richest Americans of his time. The company did not always treat its workers well. In 1892, when workers at Carnegie's Homestead mill went on strike to protest a wage cut, the strike was broken up with the

From Steel to Tech

While Pittsburgh was once known as a steel capital, today the city is thriving as a tech mecca. For instance, researchers at Carnegie Mellon University were working on driverless technology for automobiles long before those efforts became popular nationwide. That research continues, with several Pittsburgh-based companies taking the lead. Uber is using the city to test its self-driving cars. Meanwhile, Carnegie Mellon has established the CMU Robotics Institute, becoming the first university to offer a PhD in robotics.

This robotics project from Carnegie Mellon University won a national prize.

At the same time, dozens of companies and organizations have created their own small version of Silicon Valley in the heart of Pittsburgh. Companies are working on a host of creative products, including robotic baby strollers, robots that can pick and transport products from shelves, and floor-cleaning robots, to name just a few. It's no surprise that Pittsburgh has earned the nickname "Roboburgh."

Researchers say that robots won't hurt the market for human jobs. On the contrary, they believe that robots will create new, high-paying jobs, as well as making it possible for workers to greatly increase their productivity. Furthermore, they see robotics as benefiting a wide variety of industries, not just manufacturing.

aid of armed guards, and several people were killed in a fight between guards and strikers.

After he sold Carnegie Steel (for almost $500 million) in 1901, Carnegie donated hundreds of millions of dollars, largely to help establish numerous libraries, research centers, and colleges—including part of what is now Carnegie Mellon University in Pittsburgh.

Today, Pennsylvania's factories manufacture goods such as chemicals (including medicines), food products, computer and electronic products, tools, and paper. The milk from the state's dairy farms is processed and made into a variety of foods. Pennsylvania food-processing plants make cookies, cakes, crackers, bread, and other treats. The state's snack food and candy industry accounts for more than $5 billion in sales a year.

Carnegie Steel Works, 1886

Service Industries and Tourism

Service industries include banking, health care, education, retail stores, restaurants, hotels, and government. More than three-fourths of workers in Pennsylvania are employed in such industries.

Tourism is an important part of the state's economy. Millions of visitors come to Pennsylvania every year. They spend money on hotels, restaurants, and souvenirs. The tourist industry employs hundreds of thousands of Pennsylvanians.

Historic Pennsylvania draws tourists of all ages. Many travel to Philadelphia to see its colonial sites. Some sites, such as the Liberty Bell and Independence Hall (where the Declaration of Independence was approved and the Constitution was written), are located downtown in Independence National Historical Park.

FAST FACT
To celebrate the one-hundredth anniversary of the Kiss in 2007, the Hershey Company created a giant Kiss that weighed more than 30,000 pounds (13,608 kg). That Kiss holds the Guinness world record for the "world's largest piece of chocolate."

Bubble Gum: A Pennsylvania Invention

From Benjamin Franklin's bifocals to Hershey's Kisses, Pennsylvania has been the site of many interesting inventions over the years. One invention that most people have enjoyed at one time or another is bubble gum. In 1906, Philadelphia's Fleer Corporation invented the world's first bubble gum. However, it didn't work very well. It was sticky and broke apart too easily. As a result, it wasn't marketed for more than twenty years.

Then, in 1928, company employee Walter Diemer stumbled upon a new recipe. This version was sticky and allowed people to blow big pink bubbles. The gum, known as "Dubble Bubble," dominated the market for many years. It remains popular nearly a century later. The original gum came only in pink. Now it comes in a wide variety of colors and flavors.

In the 1990s, a Canadian company acquired Dubble Bubble. Now the brand is owned by Tootsie Roll Industries, which certainly knows a thing or two about sweets.

Civil War enthusiasts visit **Gettysburg**. One of the worst disasters in US history is the focus of the Johnstown Flood National **Memorial** in South Fork and the Flood **Museum** in Johnstown. Pennsylvania's rich railroad history is highlighted at places such as **Scranton's** Steamtown National Historic Site, which has one of the biggest collections of historic locomotives and rail cars in the United States.

Pennsylvania is home to many other **museums** and historical centers. Some of the best known are located in Philadelphia. These include the Franklin Institute (devoted to science), the Insectarium (for insect lovers), and the Philadelphia Museum of Art. Pittsburgh also has several popular and well-respected **museums**, including the Carnegie Museum of **Natural** History, the Carnegie Museum of Art, and the Fort Pitt Museum. Architect Frank **Lloyd** **Wright's** Fallingwater, one of his most famous houses, is about an hour outside of Pittsburgh.

Pennsylvania's famous snack food industry is centered in the southeastern part of the state. Lovers of chips and pretzels are drawn to the many factory tours in York and Lancaster Counties. The world's largest chocolate **factory** is located in Hershey. The **Hershey** Company was established in 1894, when **Milton** Hershey, its founder, opened a candy plant in Lancaster. Tourists come to Hershey to learn about and sample the company's sweet treats. Visitors also spend time at the Hershey theme park, garden, wildlife park, and spa.

Professional sports are popular—and big **business**—in the state. Many Major League Baseball fans in Pennsylvania root for the Philadelphia Phillies or the Pittsburgh Pirates. **When** football season arrives, fans cheer for the Pittsburgh Steelers or the Philadelphia Eagles

History buffs enjoy visiting Independence National Historical Park in Philadelphia.

Steamtown National Historic Site in Scranton celebrates the important role trains played in the development of the United States.

The Carnegie Museums in Pittsburgh draw visitors from all over.

The Pittsburgh Penguins have won the Stanley Cup five times, including in 2016 and 2017.

of the National Football League. In the National Hockey League, the Philadelphia Flyers and Pittsburgh Penguins skate for Pennsylvania's two largest cities. In professional basketball, the state has the Philadelphia 76ers of the National Basketball Association.

People are also drawn to Pennsylvania's wilderness. With more than 2.1 million acres (850,000 ha) of state forests, the Allegheny National Forest, and more than one hundred state parks, Pennsylvania is a haven for people who want to enjoy nature. Many families spend vacations amid the woods of the Poconos. The Delaware Water Gap National Recreation Area spans a 40-mile (64 km) stretch of the Delaware River, along the border of Pennsylvania and New Jersey. Visitors can enjoy swimming, fishing, canoeing, kayaking, and rafting, as well as hiking in the hills alongside the river.

A Bright Future

Pennsylvania's economy has been constantly evolving since the first settlers arrived nearly five hundred years ago. Originally based on farming and trade, the economy later focused on industries such as steel and coal. While the economy was originally based on farming and trade, it later turned to industries such as steel and coal. Manufacturing is still responsible for a significant amount of the state's gross domestic product (GDP), but it is no longer the leading industry. In 2017, Pennsylvania generated a GDP of

FAST FACT

The Crayola company, headquartered in Easton, makes three billion crayons each year. This is enough crayons to circle the world six times. Crayola's Easton plant produces 650 crayons per minute. The favorite crayon color among people in the United States is blue. The Crayola Experience is also a popular tourist attraction for all ages.

$752 billion. That ranked sixth among all states.

As manufacturing became less important, Pennsylvania found other ways to make money. In 2017, the state's largest industry was finance, insurance, real estate, rental, and leasing, which accounted for 19.4 percent of the state's GDP. Professional and business services ranked second, accounting for 12.6 percent of the GDP. Technology and tourism are also important contributors to state GDP. Tech industries are flourishing, especially in Pittsburgh. Meanwhile, more than 140 million tourists visit the state each year. This ranks fifth among all states nationwide.

The Allegheny National Forest offers hiking, camping, fishing, and more.

The Pennsylvania State Capitol was completed in 1906.

5 Government

When William Penn established his new colony in 1681, he wanted the people who lived there to have a say in how they were governed. The Frame of Government that he prepared helped create the democracy that the US established a hundred years later. Today, Pennsylvania is a key "swing" state in presidential elections. That means that it is a very competitive state whose important electoral votes may decide the election.

Pennsylvania is represented in the US Congress in Washington, DC. Like all states, Pennsylvania has two members in the US Senate. The number of members each state has in the US House of Representatives is related to the state's population and can change after each US census is taken. As of 2018, Pennsylvania had eighteen representatives in the US House.

County and Local Government

The state is divided into sixty-seven counties. A county is made up of several cities or smaller communities, which are called boroughs

FAST FACT
Over the years, Pennsylvania has had three different state capitals. Philadelphia served as the capital during colonial times and after the American Revolution. The capital moved to Lancaster in 1799. In 1812, the capital moved to Harrisburg, where it remains today. Harrisburg is more centrally located than the previous capitals.

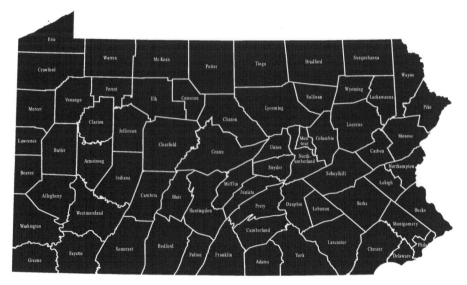

This map shows Pennsylvania's sixty-seven counties.

School districts manage the public school system.

or townships. Each county has its own government, usually run by commissioners. These commissioners handle issues that affect the many communities within the county.

However, each city, borough, or township also has its own local government. Local officials are elected by people who live in the community. Most cities and boroughs are run by a mayor and a council, or group of officials. Townships are managed by commissioners or by supervisors. City, borough, and township governments address local problems. Such issues as local budgets and land use are managed by these units of government. The public school system is managed by separate units of government called school districts.

Many Pennsylvania residents serve in local government. Some serve as officials. Many attend numerous meetings and hearings that address local problems. Through elections, in which they choose public officials and decide important issues, local residents are able to control how their community is run.

State Government

The state government is responsible for issues that affect the state as a whole. The job of state officials includes drafting, approving, and enforcing laws; managing state budgets; and handling issues between Pennsylvania and other states and between Pennsylvania and the federal government in Washington, DC.

The Governor's Residence in Harrisburg

Pennsylvania's state government is divided into three branches, which have different roles to play in governing the state. The executive branch is headed by the governor, who is the state's chief executive, or chief manager. The legislative branch passes laws for the state. The judicial branch includes the state's courts, which apply the laws to specific cases and may also decide whether a state law agrees with or violates the state constitution.

The Pennsylvania constitution explains how the state government is organized and what powers each branch of government has. The state constitution also sets **limits** on the powers of government. This **protects** the rights of individuals. Pennsylvania has changed its constitution several **times** in the course of the state's history. The current constitution was revised in **1968**.

Branches of Government

Executive

The governor is the head of the executive branch. He or she is elected to a four-year term and cannot serve more than two terms in a row. The governor's responsibilities include approving or vetoing (rejecting) proposed laws and supervising the state budget. The executive branch also includes officials who work with the governor, such as the lieutenant governor, attorney general, and state treasurer.

Legislative

The legislative—or lawmaking—branch is the Pennsylvania General Assembly. Two houses make up the assembly: the senate and the house of representatives. Senators serve four-year terms, and representatives serve for two years. There are 50 senators in the assembly and 203 representatives.

Judicial

The judicial branch is responsible for making sure that laws are followed. The state supreme court heads this branch. This court has seven justices, who are elected to ten-year terms. Lower courts include the appellate courts (the superior court and the commonwealth court), the courts of common pleas, and the community courts. These courts are often limited to certain types of cases, based on the kind of crime or other matter involved.

The Pennsylvania Judicial Center houses the commonwealth court.

How a Bill Becomes a Law

The ideas behind new laws can come from different places—sometimes from legislators and sometimes from state residents. A state resident with an idea for a law can present it to his or her state representative or senator. A proposed law is called a bill. For example, one bill might increase taxes to help pay for road repairs. Another bill might require harsh punishments for people who commit very serious crimes. Other bills define people's jobs, such as the role of volunteer firefighters.

The state senator or representative first takes their bill to the **Legislative Reference Bureau.** The bureau **writes** it in official **legal** language, **making the** bill ready for formal presentation. The bill is then given a name and number. It is first presented in the house in which it originated. This means that if a state representative helped draft the bill, it is first presented in the state house of representatives. If the bill came **from a senator,** then the presentation starts in the state senate.

Governor Tom Wolf addresses a joint session of the Pennsylvania house and senate in 2017.

The bill is introduced and then sent to a committee within the house or senate. The committee carefully studies the bill. Its job is to decide whether the bill should go to the whole house or senate to be voted on. The committee members base their decisions partly on public opinion. They may hold hearings to see how the public feels about the bill. If the committee finds that the public likes some of the ideas contained in the bill but not other parts of it, then changes—or amendments—can be made. Ultimately, the committee may decide not to send the bill to all the members of the general assembly. If a bill is rejected by the committee, it

Getting Involved

In today's fast-moving world, staying informed about government activities at the state and national level is more important than ever. Fortunately, the internet makes locating and contacting government officials easy. If you want to contact your US senator or representative, you can use Senate.gov or House.gov to locate them and find contact information. If you're not sure who your representative is, just enter your zip code.

At the state level, Pennsylvania has strived in recent years to make the government more open and transparent.

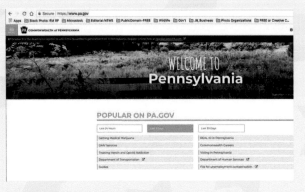

The Pennsylvania state government website is a great source of information.

The Pennsylvania government website allows you to find and contact your state legislators. Simply visit this page on the PA.gov website: https://www.pa.gov/guides/open-government. You can use a county-by-county map or type in your address.

The state government's home page also contains links to all major departments, from aging and agriculture to state police and tourism. Direct links also take visitors to the pages of the governor, lieutenant governor, attorney general, auditor general, and treasurer. All of this makes it easier than ever to learn about and be in touch with various branches and people within the government. (Make sure to ask a trusted adult before contacting anyone via phone, email, or mail!)

is said that the bill has "died in committee."

However, if the committee decides that the bill is worthy, it will send the bill to the entire house or senate for further consideration. Representatives or senators debate the bill and have a chance to suggest

amendments to it. They then vote on the bill. If the bill is passed by a majority vote, it moves on to the other half of the general assembly. There, the same process is carried out. If both houses can agree on the final bill and any amendments that were made, it is passed to the governor.

Governor Wolf signs a bill into law.

The governor reviews the bill and must decide whether to approve it or veto it. If he or she approves the bill, it becomes law. A bill that is vetoed by the governor can still become a law. For that to happen, the bill must be passed again by a two-thirds majority of each house of the general assembly.

The state encourages its residents to take an active part in their government. Many hearings are open to the public. Pennsylvanians can talk about issues that are important to them and give suggestions to their state legislators. Many legislators invite their constituents— that is, the residents they represent—to visit them at the State Capitol to learn more about the state government and its processes.

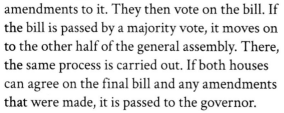

Key Issues in the Keystone State

Town meetings give Pennsylvanians a chance to speak out on important issues.

From its early reputation as the "Keystone State" during colonial days, Pennsylvania has remained a key swing state in politics. Pennsylvania's twenty electoral votes are often important in helping determine who wins the presidency.

At the state level, one of the key issues the state is facing revolves around fracking. Fracking involves injecting liquid at high pressure under Earth's surface to force open existing cracks in order to extract oil or gas. Pennsylvania ranks second in the country in terms of proved natural gas reserves. People in favor of fracking see it as an important industry for the state's economy and growth. People against fracking are worried about it damaging the environment. No matter the issue in the state, Pennsylvanians work together to make the state a wonderful place to visit and live.

Glossary

amendment	A change or addition to a legal document, such as the Constitution or a bill in the process of becoming law.
Amish	A group of people of German descent who avoid using most modern conveniences and technology. Pennsylvania's Lancaster County has a large population of Amish people.
anthracite coal	A hard coal that is plentiful in Pennsylvania.
census	An official count of the people who live in a specific area.
commonwealth	A community of people who join together to promote the common good. Pennsylvania is considered a commonwealth.
gross domestic product	The value of all the goods and services for a given year.
hydraulic fracturing	A mining technique, also called fracking, that involves breaking up rocks by shooting liquid into the ground. Hydraulic fracturing is used in Pennsylvania to harvest natural gas.
manufacturing	To make a product using machinery.
plateau	An area of relatively level high ground. Many plateaus can be found in Pennsylvania.
Quaker	A member of the Religious Society of Friends, a Christian movement founded circa 1650 and devoted to peaceful principles. William Penn, the founder of Pennsylvania, was a Quaker.

Lake Erie

Presque Isle
State Park

Erie

Warren

Bradford

Pymatuning
Reservoir

Erie National
Wildlife Refuge

Allegheny
National
Forest

East Branch
Clarion River
Reservoir

Tioga
State
Forest

Franklin

St. Marys

Susquehannock
State
Forest

Shenango
River
Lake

Maurice K.
Goddard State
Park

Clarion River

Moshannon
State
Forest

Pine Creek

Tioga River

Susquehanna River

Scranton

Delaware River

Delaware
State Forest

Sharon

Allegheny River

Sproul
State
Forest

Williamsport

Wilkes-Barre

POCONO
MOUNTAINS

New Castle

Mahoning River

Sunbury

Hazleton

Delaware
Water Gap
National
Recreation Area

Butler

Mahoning
Creek Lake

ALLEGHENY MOUNTAINS

State
College

Rothrock
State
Forest

APPALACHIAN MOUNTAINS

Little Juniata River

MOUNTAIN

JACKS

Juniata River

MONTANGO
MOUNTAIN

Susquehanna River

Hickory
Run
State Park

BLUE
MOUNTAINS

Delaware River

Allentown

Bethlehem

Pittsburgh

Altoona

Johnstown

Tuscarora
State
Forest

Reading

Schuylkill River

Harrisburg

Valley Forge
National
Historical
Park

Washington

Raystown
Lake

APPALACHIAN MOUNTAINS

Buchanan
State
Forest

TUSCARORA MOUNTAINS

KITTATINNY MOUNTAIN

Gifford Pinchot
State Park

Philadelphia

Uniontown

Forbes
State
Forest

Mount
Davis

Buchanan
State
Forest

Buchanan's
Birthplace
State Park

Chambersburg

SOUTH
MOUNTAINS

Susq. River

Lancaster

York

Delaware River

Forbes
State
Forest

Gettysburg
National
Military
Park

Gettysburg

N
W E
S

Interstate
Highway

State
Capital

Highest Point
in the State

State
Forest

Military
Park

U.S. Highway

City or Town

Mountains

State Park

Historic
Park

Pennsylvania
Turnpike

Wildlife Refuge

National Forest

Recreation Area

miles
0   20

Map Skills

1. What is the northernmost city or town?

2. What river is west of Scranton?

3. Which state forest is south of Uniontown?

4. What is the highest point in the state?

5. What city is south of Bradford?

6. Which interstate runs east to west across the state?

7. What point of interest is closest to Hazelton?

8. What river runs along Pennsylvania's eastern border?

9. What direction is Bethlehem from Philadelphia?

10. What mountain range is east of State College?

Answers

1. Erie
2. Susquehanna River
3. Forbes State Forest
4. Mount Davis
5. St. Marys
6. I-80
7. Hickory Run State Park
8. Delaware River
9. North
10. Appalachian Mountains

More Information

Books

Graves, Will. *Pittsburgh Steelers*. NFL Up Close.
    North Mankato, MN: ABDO, 2016.

Kellaher, Karen. *Pennsylvania*. True Books: My United
    States. New York: Scholastic, 2018.

Mattern, Joanne. *The Liberty Bell: History's Silent Witness*.
    South Egremont, MA: Red Chair Press, 2017.

Websites

Family-Friendly Attractions in Pennsylvania
https://visitpa.com/media/story-idea/family-
friendly-attractions-pennsylvania
Read a round-up of fun places for families to visit in Pennsylvania.

Kids' Corner: Pennsylvania State Capitol
http://www.pacapitol.com/keystone-classroom/kids-corner
Take a Pennsylvania state history quiz, complete a
crossword, print coloring pages, and more!

Pennsylvania Department of Conservation and Natural Resources
https://www.dcnr.pa.gov/StateParks/Pages/default.aspx
Learn about Pennsylvania's parks and trails on this website
hosted by the Pennsylvania state government.

Index

Page numbers in **boldface** refer to images. Entries in **boldface** are glossary terms.